MAKE
MILLIONS
on
YouTube

MAHESH DUTT SHARMA

PRABHAT
PAPERBACKS

Published by
PRABHAT PAPERBACKS
An imprint of Prabhat Prakashan Pvt. Ltd.
4/19 Asaf Ali Road,
New Delhi-110002 (INDIA)
e-mail: prabhatbooks@gmail.com

ISBN 978-93-5521-138-5
MAKE MILLIONS ON YOUTUBE
by Mahesh Dutt Sharma

Edition
First, 2022

Price
₹ 250 (Rupees Two Hundred Fifty Only)

Printed at
Sanjay Printers, Sahibabad

Author's Note

Plenty of resources, today, are available for making money on the Internet, and myriads of people around the world are exploiting these means, from the comfort of their home, to make millions.

Writing, translation, editing, proofreading, photography, H R services, virtual calling, web developing, travel agent, data entry, online tuition, blogging, domain trading, online survey, technical services, earning by reading emails, online gaming, online selling, etc., come under the purview of popular and effective means of making money online.

Besides the above, an extremely attractive way that has emerged lately to earn money online is to create your own videos and sell them on your very own YouTube channel. This involves all the Gen Z ingredients—creativity, thrill, name, fame, and money. Nobody knows which of your videos would fascinate the audience and go viral with billions of views making you a star overnight.

If content is something that excites you, go make our Youtube channel right away. With quality and consistency, success is bound to knock on your door.

This book shall serve as a guide in making you a Youtube sensation. It contains everything from the baby steps for creating a channel to rightly using Youtube to earn millions. This book is written in the simplest language and can be used by anyone irrespective of their age or background.

We wish you luck with the book. The sky is waiting for you!

❑❑❑

Contents

Author's Note 3

1. Who Wants to Be a YouTube Millionaire? 7
2. Create YouTube Channel and Make Millions 21
3. Making a Hit Video 39
4. Most Popular YouTube Channels 46
5. Perfect Name for YouTube Channel 55
6. YouTube Channel and Description 63
7. Be a YouTube Earning Wizard 67
8. Perfect Topic for YouTube Channel 78
9. Video Content and Quality 96
10. Earning Faces on YouTube Channels 100
11. Farmers Earning Millions on YouTube 106

Addendum: Other Sources for Online Income 108

1

Who Wants to Be a YouTube Millionaire?

You must have often come across interesting videos on the social media site, YouTube. Do you know that every time you view a complete video, the chances of earning by the channel you viewed the video on gets boosted? Likewise, you can also earn millions by making videos on YouTube, provided you have a real zest for it.

The youth is quite fascinated and indulged in using social media sites to create content and, thereafter, making millions from uploading them. According to *Forbes*, 26-year-old Felix Kjellberg is making billions just from his YouTube channel PewDiePie. In line, there is Roman Atwood's channel. The number of its subscribers has grown to around 10,155,036. Roman Atwood manages to stay in the limelight by creating hilarious prank videos. He has attained an annual income of around 540 million rupees.

The charisma of Super Woman persists

Indian-origin Lilly Singh, who runs a channel by the name of 'Super Woman', comes third in the list. The number of subscribers her channel is 10,336,049. Forbes estimates her income at ₹ 500 million. Lilly is also the highest-earning woman on YouTube. Next in the line is the team of comedians, Ian and Anthony. They have 5,339,808 subscribers. The duo is able to earn around ₹ 470 million from their YouTube channel using their comic videos. They are also engaged in film production.

The fifth position in respect of earnings is secured by Tyler Oakley. The number of subscribers on his YouTube channel is 8,086,885. He earns up to ₹ 400 million through his talk shows.

Wouldn't you also like to make some money on YouTube? So come on, let me illustrate to you how you also can make a name for yourself by creating your own YouTube channel. There is a channel linked with every YouTube account. You may create your YouTube channel using your Gmail account also. You may even access this YouTube account through Google Drive. After creating your own YouTube channel, you would have to use some keywords that might make your channel search-friendly.

Upload Original Content

You will succeed in making money on YouTube only when the content of your channel is original and engaging. It is also important to ensure quality of these videos red while uploading. The size of the video content also makes a difference. Users look for content that consume minimal Internet data. The content needs to be constantly updated to attract advertisements. Choosing special keywords for each video and also keeping a watch on trending topics and new videos can help in making the uploaded content viral.

How to make Money from your YouTube videos?

If your YouTube channel is constantly attracting more and more viewers and you are getting considerable page views on the same, you should monetise the video as soon as possible to make money out of the same. Video monetisation simply means providing Google the option to run its advertisements in your video.

Monetisation of YouTube Video

For this, you need to go to the dashboard of your YouTube channel and click on the 'Monetisation' button. If you are not able to do monetisation there, another option is to go to the 'Channel Settings' page and click on 'Monetisation' tab there. You will have to then click on 'Monetise with Ad' box.

YouTube Mail brings good news

If any video on your YouTube channel is getting a large number of views, you may receive an email from YouTube. This certainly would be good news for you. The email would have details relating to the payment that YouTube would make to you for your uploaded video, however, this would be just for a specific video. In order to continue receiving advertisements, all videos would need to be individually monetised.

This is news for both kind of users—those who own their YouTube channels and those who view their favourite videos. Suppose, you run a YouTube channel and are even able to make some money with a reasonable level of subscriber base. In that case, you would be probably aware that, quite often, YouTube has to face criticisms for underpaying the users for their videos. YouTube has, hence, provided another option to the channel owners to earn money. YouTube channel owners would now be able to also charge their subscribers and viewers directly.

Paid membership

YouTube has offered its channel owners a new option to launch paid membership plans. Thus, besides earning from advertisements, YouTube channel owners would also be able to earn by selling their memberships. This feature, though, is not in favour of the viewers of YouTube videos, as they might have to shell out money before viewing a video. Channels having more than 100,000 subscribers may launch paid subscriptions for their channel membership, requiring the viewers to pay 4.99 dollars per month towards the same.

For example, if you like all the videos on a particular YouTube channel and you have subscribed to the channel, you may be asked by the channel to buy 'Channel Membership'. In that case, you would be able to view the videos on the channel only after you purchase its membership. The channels creating their own videos may even sell items like shirts and phone covers on their channels. Most channels that have now gained popularity sell their merchandise on YouTube to earn more money.

IDENTIFY YOUR TALENT

From the perspective of a creator who wants to earn millions, the basic knowledge of the Internet, camcorder, or editing, are not the only things one should learn. The first step should always be to identify your own talent. You will have to determine which kind of videos you would like to provide on your YouTube channel. Once you have finalised that, you should go ahead and create your YouTube channel.

4,000 HOURS OF WATCH TIME

YouTube has since made some changes in its policy. Earlier, YouTube required a minimum of 10,000 views to enable a channel to make money. However, as per the new policy, you need to gain a minimum of 4,000 viewing hours on your channel during the last 12 months to make money. Additionally, you must have a minimum of 1,000 subscribers. Only after you meet both criteria, you would be eligible to make money on YouTube.

45:55 REVENUE SHARE BY YOUTUBE

Out of the revenue earned on YouTube, 45 percent of the same goes to YouTube and 55 percent is given to you. This revenue comes from advertising different brands or running their advertisements on your channel. You get these advertisements only when viewership on your channel grows.

REVENUE FROM MARKETING

Advertisements are not the only source of income on a YouTube channel. There is one more way you can make money on your channel. You have the option of earning revenue by marketing a company or a person on your channel, provided of course, the channel enjoys substantial viewership and a good subscriber base. Under this, you would attach a link of the product or service (you want to market) 1 in the description box of your video. This video will have information related to that product or service. Revenue would be generated when a visitor gets redirected from your channel to the respective page through that link.

YouTube has, today, grown to be the most popular online video site in the world. We turn to YouTube first whenever we want to view some video. It reaches almost every person in the world. This is a site where anybody may enjoy his/her favorite videos.

YouTube was launched 14 February 2005, on the occasion of Valentine's Day. An interesting fact is that YouTube was a dating site before it turned into a video streaming and viewing platform. This was founded by Chad Hurley, Steve Chen, and, Jawed Karim. All three earlier worked for PayPal. Just one and a half years after the launch of this site, the famous search engine company Google acquired it for a sum of 1.65 billion dollars. This also proved to be the largest Online deal of that time.

More than 100 hours of videos are uploaded to the site every minute. Almost 1 billion hours of videos are watched every 24 hours, i.e., every day. This is the third-largest website in the world, next only to Google and Facebook. And this is the world's second-largest search engine, next only to Google.

- Around 1.3 billion people watch videos on this site every day.
- Around 5 billion videos are watched every day on YouTube.
- 'Me at the zoo' is the first video that was uploaded to YouTube, featuring the site's co-founder Jawed Karim at San Diego Zoo. This video was uploaded on 23 April, 2005.
- Women constitute almost 38 percent of the users in this largest video-sharing website in the world.
- People spend an average of 40 minutes per day on the YouTube website.
- ' PewDiePie' with a subscriber base of over 55,400,000, is the largest channel on YouTube.
- In India, 'T-Series' is the largest channel having 24,465,720 subscribers.
- PSY's video 'Gangnam Style', with a view count of around 2.86 billion, is the most-viewed video on YouTube.
- YouTube is available in 76 languages across 89 countries.
- It made a total earning of 8.5 billion dollars in 2015; this is expected to grow to 27.4 billion dollars by the year 2020.
- YouTube website domain became active on 14 February 2005, though the website was further developed later.

Largest video sharing website

YouTube is the largest video-sharing website where you can upload your videos relating to any subject. Not only that, you may even make money out of those videos. However, there was no intention to make money by uploading videos when this website was originally created. Before YouTube was launched, there did exist some other websites where videos could be uploaded. However,YouTube provided a different interface for uploading and sharing videos that behave made the site so popular today. The Internet has many websites also, other than YouTube, relating to different subjects that have become immensely popular, Facebook, Google, and Twitter being some of them.

Out of the above websites, YouTube is the one that is being used the most around the world, People rely on YouTube for basically everything- information, entertainment, learning, laughing- just name it!

History and evolution of YouTube

The Internet came into existence in 1990 and the first website was launched on the Internet in 1991. The first search engine became operational in 1990 and people started using the same for searching on the Internet. Availability of the search engine helped generate awareness among people about the Internet. Later in 1998, Google created its own search engine that eliminated most of the search-related issues and provided a very convenient tool for people to look for any information on the Internet.

PayPal was founded around the same time the search engine was launched by Google in 1998. Chad Hurley, Steve Chen, and Jawed Karim were working for PayPal. The trio got together to develop an Online dating site and launch a new company. The company was named 'Tune in, Hook up'. The purpose of this website was to enable anybody to upload his/her video to the Internet. Other users could watch the video and decide whether to hook up with that person. However, this idea failed miserably. The process did not click with its users.

In 2005, this trio after tasting failure in their first venture, noticed that there was no video-sharing website on the Internet. Jawed Karim had found it very difficult in 2004 to view the video clips of the Janet Jackson incident that occurred during the Super Bowl and the Indian Ocean tsunami on the Internet. Keeping this very issue in mind, the three thought about building something that could not only allow people to view videos comfortably on the Internet but also make the search for specific videos easy and convenient. And that was the idea behind the conceptualization and creation of the YouTube website by this trio.

THE JOURNEY OF YOUTUBE

YouTube was first launched on 14 February 2005 and it was on 23 April 2005 when the first video of just 18 seconds, named 'Me at the zoo', was created for users on its beta version. This video is available on Jawed Karim's channel on YouTube even today. This very video had received the first comment.

In September 2005, a Nike ad became the first video to reach one million views. In November 2005, Sequoia Capital was the first to fund YouTube for 3.5 million dollars. YouTube was formally launched for the public in December 2005. Sensing the popularity of YouTube on the Internet, Google acquired the same in 2006 for 1.65 million dollars. All 67 employees working for YouTube at that time were now working for Google. In May 2007, YouTube launched its 'Partner Programme' that allowed creators to demonstrate their talent, courage, and skill on YouTube and also make money. In July 2007, YouTube hosted the US presidential debate in collaboration with CNN.

Vevo music video service was launched in 2009 and movie rental service was launched in 2010. A substantial number of videos started getting quite popular in 2010. When Olympic Games was held in London in 2012, YouTube had streamed all the games live and had also played a significant role in publicising and promoting the 2012 Olympic Games. It was in 2012 only when the song video 'Gangnam Style' reached 1 billion views. YouTube recorder was originally 32-bit based and was upgraded to 64-bit after the launch of the song video 'Gangnam Style'.

Initially, viewing YouTube videos required the installation of Adobe Flash Player software. However, YouTube in 2015 started HTML5 video playback services that did away with that requirement. With the change of time, YouTube kept upgrading itself and a number of improvements in video quality were also implemented with features like 3D video, 360-degree video, YouTube Red, and YouTube TV.

Income from Advertisements

YouTube earns from its advertisements. Ads are inserted in videos uploaded by creators and these ads only generate income. Even today, YouTube is striving to provide the best of services to its users. We may see still better features on YouTube in the coming days. YouTube is getting immensely popular and people now find it quite convenient to view any video on this site.

YouTube allows its registered users to upload, view, and share videos, link, report and comment on favourite videos and take up membership of channels of other users. Videos belonging to its members as well as many well-known companies are available on this site. These videos include clips, TV programmes, music videos, movie trailers, and live streaming. Some people use this as a video blogging site also. Non-registered users can only view videos whereas registered users may even upload unlimited videos and comment on others' videos. Some videos like those promoting contempt, exploitation, nudity, and crime and those detrimental to people below 18 years of age are available for viewing only to registered users over 18 years of age.

YouTube earns money through Google AdSense which serves its advertisements based on site contents and users. Under this, most of the videos may be watched free of cost, though some of them may require payment. Such paid services include a movie rental service wherein you may watch a movie Online after making the required payment. You may even subscribe to YouTube Premium membership that allows you to view videos free of advertisements. Besides, there are some videos on the site that you can view only as a member of the YouTube Premium service.

There is now plenty of people earning name and money on YouTube. Nobody knows which of the videos would attract viewers. There are plenty of examples where channel owners, after facing a lot of problems initially, were well received by the users of the site.

Everything, right from cooking tips to songs, music,

films, and tips for home remedies is available at the site. It would be quite unusual if you do not get a positive search result for anything that you are looking for on the site.

❑

2

Create YouTube Channel and Make Millions

YouTube can be accessed in different ways depending upon the need of the user. You may use your Google account to subscribe to YouTube channels, view their videos, and even like them. However, this way restricts you to only being a viewer and you do not have any sole identity on YouTube. You would need a YouTube channel to be able to upload videos and comments and to create video playlists. You may use a computer (to access the YouTube website) or mobile (to access YouTube mobile site) to create a new channel.

- Sign in to YouTube using a computer or a mobile.
- Perform steps required for your channel like uploading videos, writing reviews, or creating video playlists.
- If you don't own a channel, you will be provided an option to create a channel.

- Ensure that the details (like Google account name, photo, etc.) submitted for creating your channel are entered correctly and confirm channel creation.

Channel with a Commercial Name

Please follow the instructions below for creating a channel that may be owned or managed by more than one individual. You may use a brand account for creating such a channel. The channel may have a different name but may still be managed through your Google account.

- Sign in to YouTube using a computer or mobile.
- Go to your channel list.
- Choose to create a new channel or use any existing brand account.
- Click on the option 'Create New Channel' and create your new channel.
- Select the brand account that you are already managing and create a YouTube channel for the same. You will not be able to create a new channel if a channel already exists for the brand. If you select the brand account in the list, you would be able to switch to that brand channel only.
- Enter all the information required for opening the channel and confirm. Click on 'Done' after that. This would create a new brand channel.

- To add a channel manager, follow the instructions for modifying channel owners and managers.

Channel creation

Go to the YouTube site and log in with your Google account. Once logged in, you would find your name or username on the top of the menu on the left side. Click on the same to access your user page.

Upload artwork for the channel. This is the channel art that would be displayed on the top of your channel page. YouTube would provide some examples of how that channel art would be displayed on various devices.

- Use an artwork capable of attracting the attention of your viewers. The look of your cover would make e-viewer decide if he/she wants to hop onto your channel. Therefore, creating artwork that can be easily distinguished from other channels is very important. Include your name or a tagline in the channel art. This would help viewers in remembering your name and coming back to your channel.
- Change your channel art on regular basis. You needn't do the same if you plan to establish the image of your brand by maintaining the same artwork. Otherwise, you should go about altering your channel art regularly based on the contents posted on your channel. Thus,

if you are uploading comedy videos, your channel art should match the theme of comedy.

Describe your channel

Provide a brief introduction to your channel; this would help viewers guess the kind of videos you are going to upload. To incorporate the same on your channel, go to the 'About' tab in the main window of your channel and then click on the button there.

Name your channel

Look into the description of your channel and consider the kind of videos you propose to upload while naming your channel. The name should be short, simple, and easy to remember.

Search for popular videos on YouTube

The first step towards uploading your video is to determine what you wish to share with the world. People use YouTube for different purposes like viewing music videos for relaxing, comedy videos for enjoyment,tutorial videos for learning, amongst many other activities. Hence, give thoughts to decide what unique content you could come up with that other channels are not already serving to the viewers.

Determine your talent

Passion helps in keeping the inside fire burning. Consider making comedy videos if your friends maintain that you are a fun-loving person. If you love singing, try out a video with you as the singer. Keep uploading videos that continue to draw viewers' attention and also makes you happy.

Consider writing reviews

Writing product reviews is an excellent way of gaining views, especially if you are reviewing an item that people are looking for. People do tend to view reliable reviews of the products or services they plan to buy. There are plenty of subjects that may be picked for review, like:

- New albums
- Latest appliances
- TV and films
- Video games
- Books
- Restaurants and other food products
- Businesses

Content... the more, the better

Continue striving to create more and more content for your viewers. Not only would this keep your viewers interested in your channel but also help you hone your skills over time. Patience and persistency is the key.

Work on basic techniques

If you are speaking on the camera, make sure that the camera is fixed and you are speaking clearly and in a steady tone. You may be trying to make the world's most interesting video, but if you are not properly presentable or audible, nobody would like to view that video. Therefore, small things matter a lot.

Practise video editing

Rather than an amateurish video made in a hurry, a well-edited video would make a much better impact on your viewers. Spend some time learning your video editing software. You may even go through Online tutorials to learn basic editing techniques. There are many free and open-source video editing software available on the Internet. Many of these software have similar features that costly commercial editing software boast of. The audience appreciates efforts and clarity.

Make introduction fascinating

Most of the viewers evaluate a video in the first few seconds of the same. Strive to make your introduction entertaining and informative. The longer your video is watched by the viewers, the higher the same would be positioned by YouTube in its search results.

Show a preview of the video that the viewer is going to watch. Please ensure that you are in focus right from the start of the video. Talk to the viewers directly. Present the video yourself and talk about the video briefly. There is no need to explain the video in detail.

If you have created a brand like your name or a serial that you have produced, ensure that the opening of the video is done professionally.

While creating a real-life video like a review or tutorial, ensure that the purpose of the video is clear right from the beginning, else the viewer would look for another video relating to the subject.

Therefore, the introduction should be short and crisp with a quick highlight overviewing what is inside. This will ensure growth and also make it effective for the audience who is watching.

Focus on Advertisements

Media keeps on advertising various happenings in almost all sectors round the year. These are called 'Events'. Reflect on the same and determine which kind of events might attract your viewers.

Consider making videos for upcoming events. As the curiosity grows for the event, more and more people would look for content relating to the event. While the event is on, make videos relating to the same. These videos would be useful for the viewers who are unable to personally experience the event.

Once the event is over, make a video containing a summary of the same. Cover briefly all the activities of the event in this video and analyse all the available details. Interact with your viewers during the process to keep them glued to your channel. During big events, augment the number of your videos in order to gain fresh viewers. A good number of videos would make viewers feel that you are quite knowledgeable and enthusiastic about the event. Making vlogs and raw videos is also what can help you keep your audience hooked on your content.

Tell a story

You need to present a story in every video—be it a real-life subject or an imaginary content. It should have a briefing beginning, involving central part, and a specific end. Every video should tell a story even if it is a comedy video or a tutorial on taking care of flowers.

Break your long videos into small parts—each part focusing on a specific aspect of the subject. This would make the subject more understandable and interesting for the viewers. Ensure that there is not a lot of repetition and your video does not get boring for your audience.

Use of Annotations

There are text boxes displayed in your videos. Use them for redirecting viewers to other videos, channels, and external websites.

- You may use annotations to prompt your viewers to subscribe to your channel.
- Use annotations to redirect viewers from your old videos to new videos.
- Annotations may act as a 'List of Content' for a long video and you may even use the same to lead a viewer to a specific time in the video.

Constant Updates

If you have earned fame on the strength of your theatrical work, you should speak to your viewers by dedicating a full episode wherein you may respond to popular questions raised through comments and talk about the methodology of your creativity. Such backstage videos would help you connect well with your viewers and you would be able to demonstrate that they do make a lot of impact on your work.

If you wish to control who could or could not view your video, you may click on the 'Privacy' drop-down menu and select 'Private'. You may then enter the names or email IDs of those YouTube users to whom you want to provide access. You may send 50 private invitations for each video.

If you want to upload videos longer than 15 minutes, you will need to verify your account with Google.

Creative tags

Adding tags to your video helps viewers find your content. You should ensure that your tags are connected to the video and at the same time, ensure that you are not using the tags that are not being used by other channel owners for the same category of videos.

While thinking of tags, try to keep the same concise. For instance, instead of adding multiple tags to your video, it would a better idea to use a few but exceptional tags. Add the tags that people generally use to search for such videos. Your tags should reflect well the contents of the video. Try to blend both comprehensiveness and uniqueness in a single tag.

You may use tags to create sections of your video. Use a unique tag and use the same for all videos that you plan to keep together. Thus, more and more people would be able to watch all of your videos and will enjoy a friendly interface.

Maintenance of Your Channel

Keep uploading videos—yes, if you want to make your channel successful, you need to keep uploading new videos. Strive to update your channel at least once every two weeks. If you are not going to upload videos for some time, you should keep your viewers informed of the same and also let them know when you plan to resume uploading videos. Your audience should be like your family which is regularly updated on how are you being.

Regular video uploads may help you improve the number of your viewers. Think of this as a TV show; everybody eagerly awaits a new episode of his favourite show and he/she knows when the next episode is expected. Try to upload new videos every week or every alternate week. Be consistent and regular.

Interaction with Viewers

As and when you get time, you should try to respond to the comments of your viewers. This would help create a strong connection between you and your viewers. When the viewers feel you care for them, they would keep coming back to your channel, watch your videos and even recommend your channel to others.

After uploading a video, spend a few hours responding to the comments of your viewers on that video. These viewers are your best followers as they impatiently await your new videos and even shower comments on them. Respect them and then watch the number of your viewers grow.

Try to scrutinize as many comments as possible on your channel. Going through negative comments may not be amusing sometimes as they tarnish the image of your channel and even your regular viewers feel displeased with that. Delete the comments that disgrace others and report such delinquent users. This would help in creating a favourable environment for your regular viewers.

You may even raise questions for the viewers to answer. Try to keep your questions simple like those having Yes/No answers or 'Voting' questions. This would reduce negative remarks and promote healthy discussion among viewers. The viewers will feel inclusive and will like to regularly visit your channel to stay updated.

Bring back old videos

If you have old videos that your current viewers might not have viewed, you may include the same in your feed. This would allow everybody to view the same on your channel and thus, even your old videos would get added viewership.

Keep watching other channels

Continue with the YouTube channel as long as possible, even if you are not uploading any content on your channel. Watch others' videos, talk to other users and search for appropriate videos and view them.

Provide a link to any other user's video that looks similar to your video. This would make your video appear along with the related video on the for you page of the user.

Make a schedule for linking other videos. During the days when you are not uploading your videos, you may review the videos that you have linked and liked. This would help you reduce the waiting period between your video uploads and also keep your viewers active on your channel.

While liking a video on any other channel, you should ensure that the selected video is capable of properly attracting the attention of your viewers. You should take care not to upset your viewers by admiring a video that has not been liked by anybody else or which might hurt the sentiments of your viewers.

Show your viewers' videos

Try to incorporate commentaries and works of your viewers in your videos. Create a signpost for presentation, like the requirement to subscribe to your channel.

Look for collaboration with other users. Connect with the people who are involved in uploading videos in the same category that you do. Promoting each other's channels would help increase the number of viewers. Try to present yourself on others' videos and also invite others to appear in your videos.

Ensure that your viewers can easily visit the channels with whom you are working. Your viewers should get fully immersed in videos created by your community.

Maintaining connections and then using them can really help in networking and reaching masses.

Use of social media

Link the videos and playlists of your channel on Facebook, Google, Twitter and other social media. Request your friends to share links to your videos with others—online or offline.

Avoid spamming your social media network by posting links to your channel. A small reminder may be ok, but rarely would anybody react positively if you keep posting the link to your channel repeatedly.

It should be a combination of not being too much and not too less. You should ensure that you are making aware people of your channel and in the process not boring them.

Channel promotion

Request your viewers to publicise your channel. You should not do this constantly; instead, you may appeal to share the link to your video if they like the same. This message should be conveyed towards the end of your video after the viewer has gone through the main content. You may also remind the viewers to 'Like' your video and 'Subscribe' to your channel if they have not already.

IGNORING NEGATIVITY

Be careful while choosing the name for the channel you are creating. You would not be able to change the same later. Pick a name that describes your channel's topic, that is unique, that people can easily remember and that is different from the names other YouTube users have used. Investigate and ensure that the name that you have picked is available and the same is not similar to a name that somebody else has already used.

You should have a good understanding of the video that you are going to upload. People may find your channel a bit peculiar if you upload a video with content that you are not familiar with.

You may sometimes receive a few negative comments, but you should better ignore them and continue your work. However, take care not to disregard creative criticism as a negative remark. A viewer's critique of any part of your video should be used to make your next video better. It should not be something that you take so much seriously or degrade your confidence thereafter.

Please ensure that your video follows all the terms and conditions of YouTube. If any of your videos violates the terms of YouTube, the same may be removed and your account may even get restricted. Hence, ensure that all the content that you upload meet the requirements of YouTube.

Interesting: Made millions on YouTube

A six-year-old South Korean YouTube star girl Boram has earned ₹ 550 million from her two YouTube channels. She has bought a 5-storey property in Seoul, the capital city. The property is situated on a 258-square-metre plot of land. This is being used by Boram's family. There are more than 30 million subscribers on her YouTube channels.

Boram's first channel is a toy review channel. It has 13.6 million subscribers. The other channel is a video blog having 17.6 million subscribers. Boram uploads videos relating to her family's daily life on this channel. Her YouTube channels are the most popular ones in South Korea.

The two channels together have become the highest-grossing channel group of the country. One user has remarked that even during his entire life, he would not have earned the income that Boram has made on YouTube in a single year.

An idea of Boram's popularity may be made from the fact that her one video had attracted 370 million views.

The video shows Boram briskly cooking noodles and then suddenly spilling the same.

Boram has also been in controversies relating to her videos. The case relating to one of her clips had even landed in court. In that clip released in the year 2017, Boram was seen explaining to her viewers how she had stolen money from her father's wallet. She then attempts to drive a car. This incident resulted in the family court summoning Boram's parents and ordering them to send Boram to a counseling centre.

The record of a child making the highest earnings on YouTube is held by seven-year-old Ryan of the United States of America. He has earned over 1.52 billion rupees from his toy channel which boasts over 20.8 million subscribers.

YouTube is not only a means of making money online but also provides a platform for people to demonstrate their talent. Many people are using YouTube to make millions every month. Some have even made this their full-time career.

You may include your social media profiles on your YouTube channel. This would help the visitors to your channel find your Facebook and Twitter accounts easily. This provides trustworthiness to your channel and make your content credible.

Do your research first

Now that you have decided to create a YouTube channel, you must first decide the genre for the same. You would gain nothing if you create a YouTube channel just like that without anything in your head. Hence, please choose your genre, do thorough research, and create your YouTube channel with proper planning and passion.

❑

3

Making a Hit Video

First of all, you must ensure that you do not upload any copyrighted content belonging to others on your YouTube channel. Your video content should be original and its video quality should be good—then only people would love to view videos on your channel.

Use simple words to name your video. Choose your content in compliance with government rules and regulations only. Make sure not to pick any content that might prompt the government or YouTube authority l to close/freeze your channel. Also, avoid using obscenity in your videos, or else your account might get blocked.

The selection of keywords plays the most vital role in making your channel videos a hit or flop. Hence, strive to create good content matching the keywords that are currently trending. Keywords help you in catching the eye of the user scrolling on YouTube by showing your videos in related or recommended area.

Make sure to do some research before you take up creating your video and pick up subjects that have not been used much.

When you view a video on YouTube, it generates some income for the concerned channel owner. The more you view that video, the more would be the earnings for the channel owner who created and uploaded that video.

You might also have heard about people making millions every year by just uploading videos on YouTube. 'BB Ki Vines', 'AIB' and 'Super Woman' are some of the YouTube channels that earn millions every year. These people have turned into celebrities today just by uploading videos and are called YouTube stars. Their work is earning for them offers from Bollywood and Hollywood too. Like them, you may also connect with YouTube to earn income. You just need an idea and some necessary resources like a camera for creating videos and you are ready to go!

The first step towards earning on YouTube is to create a channel on the platform. You may create a channel for free by logging in on the site using your Gmail account. But, before you create your channel, decide the genre on which you wish to create your videos. Once that is decided, you may give your channel a name that is unique and associated with that topic. This would help your channel get searched easily by viewers and hence, your earnings get boosted.

The first condition for making money with YouTube is to ensure that all the videos you upload are original and do not face ay copyright issues.

Monetise your channel

You may start earning on YouTube right from the first day itself. You just need to monetise your channel for the same. Monetisation entails giving YouTube permission to show ads before the start of videos on your channel. Additionally, this is also is a proof that nobody else has a copyright on the videos that you are uploading.

To initiate monetisation, you may go to Video Manager and click on the 'Enable Monetisation' or '$' sign. Tick the box relating to 'Monetise with Ads'... and you enable your chance of earning!

Link your channel with Google AdSense

Besides monetisation, Google AdSense is another default ad system that generates revenue for you constantly. Your account would get credited every time your video is viewed and every time an ad shown on your channel redirects the user on the linked website.

Sign up for Google AdSense by visiting its site. Here also, you may log in using your Gmail account. You would have to provide your bank account details or PayPal account details here.

AdSense uses your bank account or PayPal account not only for verifying your credentials but also for making payments to you. Linking your channel to AdSense would augment per-view revenue for your videos.

Advertisement for Your Channel and Videos

Just creating a channel and regularly uploading videos on the same would not earn millions for you. For that, you need to advertise your channel. Try to publicise your channel and videos through mouth publicity, on social media, and all possible platforms where you expect a potential audience. The more you gain subscribers and views, the more would be your earning. This would also help you go one step ahead of monetisation and become a YouTube partner, thus reaping other benefits.

Become YouTube Partner

Successfully establishing your channel makes you eligible to become a YouTube partner. You may visit your YouTube page and choose to become a YouTube partner anytime, but you need to meet certain terms and conditions for the same. Joining YouTube Partner Programme requires a minimum of 15,000 viewing hours on your channel during the last 90 days. Once you reach this level, you may apply for the partnership.

The partnership not only entitles you to YouTube support but also makes you eligible to win many awards. Every year, YouTube offers Golden, Orange, and Diamond Play Button awards to the best YouTube channels. These awards are offered to the channels that were able to secure many more views than others. And of course, these awards are made of gold and diamond with your name also inscribed in golden letters.

Initial Income

Before deciding to go ahead with launching your channel on YouTube, you must understand that for attaining a revenue level of millions on the same, you would have to have patience for some time and continue improving your work till your good is better and your better is the best. In the beginning, when you monetise your videos and link to AdSense, you get something from 25 paise to one rupee per click. You may multiply this income many times by increasing your channel views.

For making money on YouTube, the above are the two ways that enable you to earn even with zero subscribers and less than 1,000 views. But to make millions and billions on YouTube, you will have to wait for some time and keep uploading quality content consistently.

Way to Make Millions

If you want to earn millions every year, you need to give a year or more to yourself. During that period, keep your focus away from earning, and only on making your channel better and still better.

Do whatever you can to augment your subscriber base as well as views. The more popular your channel becomes, the more number of brands would prefer to collaborate with you.

Most of the companies offer the option to endorse their products on YouTube channels with subscriber base and views running in thousands and millions. These advertising deals may earn you millions every month, but that is possible only when you make your channel so attractive and popular that everybody wants to view the same.

Mistakes that may cost you dearly

If you are thinking of clicking on the ads appearing in your videos to augment your earnings, then beware, that may cost you dearly. If you indulge in clicking those ads in your videos repeatedly and YouTube finds anything fishy in the same, your AdSense account may get canceled.

As far as possible, keep your contents original. You will not be able to earn anything on copyrighted content. Hence, keep everything—right from photos to music and other contents original.

Never upload any video that is controversial or indecent or that may harm anybody. YouTube scans all the videos uploaded on its site. A video may get removed if any inappropriate content is found in the same. If this happens repeatedly, your channel runs the risk of getting blocked.

Originality is something you need to ensure if you want to be the horse of the long run. You should also make sure that by uploading videos, you are adding some value to your channel. Videos should not just be uploaded because of the sake of doing it, but it should also make some sense.

This is how to make copyright-free video

If you wish to incorporate some music, photos, or video footage in your video and you are short of funds for the same, instead of worrying, head to these resources.

For music, there is a YouTube audio library where different kinds of copyright-free music are available. Besides, there are plenty of websites like incompetech.com that provide music for free. There are also many websites like pixabay.com where copyright-free photos and videos are available. You may pick photos and videos from there as per your requirements and use them without any issues.

You must, however, keep in mind that whenever you use copyright-free content, you must give credits for that content at the end of your video or at any other part of the same. If you fail to do so, you may invite claims from the respective site for copyright infringement.

❑

4

Most Popular YouTube Channels

You should start your YouTube channel with the topic that you are most conversant with or that is close to your heart. Such a channel generally has greater chances to succeed.

Besides the above, tutorial videos, teaching, and some problem-solving videos are widely watched. Gadget reviews and fashion-related tips are some of the topics that are searched the most on YouTube.

However, launch your channel on a topic that you love and that excites you. You cannot make big out of it, if you are not passionate about it. You would be able to run such a channel in a better way and also put in the required effort for the same. Keep uploading your videos on a regular basis. This would help attract more subscribers and improve earnings with better views.

Important points

If you take YouTube seriously, you may even make this your full time career. Lilly Singh of 'Super Woman' is a typical example. She earns millions every year just by creating YouTube videos.

You can't make millions on YouTube overnight. Just as business takes time to establish and reach break-even, this also takes time. Hence, you need to be patient and keep uploading videos. Regular upload of videos would help you turn your earnings from thousands to millions.

You have, then, a fair chance to make 'one day' to 'day one'.

Connect with your audience

One point that needs to be essentially kept in mind before launching a channel is to consider what kind of content you are going to present to your audience and whether your content involves your audience. Quite often, a YouTube channel fails to succeed despite serving excellent content and that happens because of the lack of involvement of the audience with the content. Your audience itself becomes a family which wants a two-way relationship where they are investing their time and interest into you in return for some response from you as well.

Logo/Icon

A user on the Internet pays more attention to visuals than to the text of a site. You must have an icon or logo before you start a channel; this would be the symbol of your work everywhere. It should be something you want to be recognised by.

Channel art

This is kind of a cover photo. If a user likes your video, he would surely visit your channel at least once. Hence, it's necessary that you wonderfully welcome the visitor. Channel art is the first thing visitors see when they visit your channel. So, it's an important part of making a long-lasting first impression on someone who has come to yur channel.

Share content

Besides providing good content on your channel, its marketing is also equally important. It is like you have made the best content out there, but still you need people to watch and appreciate it. Hence, it's important to promote your content properly on different social media platforms. This would help your channel gain popularity among the public in a better way and reach masses.

YouTube channel on mobile

If you are well educated and still not able to secure a job, you need not wait for the same idly. Instead, you may take up work Online to make money. However, the best and easiest thing to make most of that time is to upload good informative videos to YouTube. You may even create and upload videos related to your own academic knowledge; that may help others and, in return, earn you some income. And the best thing about this is that this does not require any investment. You may create your YouTube channel for free and start uploading your videos there.

Uploading videos

YouTube has recently implemented some limitations under which, you can start earning from videos on your channel only after achieving 4,000 view hours. Hence, you should keep uploading videos to your channel. A few good videos would very soon gain 4,000 view hours and help you start earning income.

You will need a YouTube App. to create your channel through mobile. If you don't have the YouTube App., you may download the same from Google Play Store. Once downloaded, you install and open the same.

On opening the App., you get the 'Account' option. Clicking the same opens the' Sign in' screen. You have to sign in using this option.

On clicking the 'Sign in' option, you can see a '+' icon next to 'Account'. If you have already logged in with your email ID, that ID also is displayed here. If you wish to run your YouTube channel using the same email ID, you can continue to do so by simply login in via that ID. Otherwise, you can create a new account by clicking the '+' icon.

Successful login or new account creation takes you to the home screen. Click on the 'Account' icon again and then select the 'My Channel' option. You can see a head asking 'your name'.Here, you need to enter the name of your YouTube channel and click on the 'Channel' option.

Now you have to adjust the settings for your channel. For this, click on the 'Settings' icon and add your logo and back cover for your channel. Both the items are quite necessary. Your channel would not look professional in their absence. Hence, do add a logo or a photo for your channel first.

Next, you may change the name of your channel again. Below the same, you have to provide a description for your channel. The description should cover the purpose of your channel, the topic on which you would be creating your videos, etc. Once done, the process of creating a YouTube channel through mobile is over.

Uploading videos on YouTube using a phone

In order to upload videos on YouTube using Android app on your phone, you need to click on the 'Video' icon. Clicking this will show an another video icon which now needs to be clicked. It will, then, display all the videos available on your phone. Select the video you wish to upload.

- Enter the name of your video.
- Write about the video—what the video contains and how its unique.
- If you keep the video 'Public', anybody can view it. If you make this 'Private', only you will be able to view it.. If marked 'Unlisted', only the people whom you send its link would be able to view the video.

Click on the 'Upload' icon after completing all information. This will upload the selected video to YouTube. You may upload your other videos using the above process.

Uploading videos on YouTube using computer

First of all, go to the YouTube site using your browser and click on the Sign in option on the right side. You need to log in here using your Gmail ID. Once logged in, click on the 'Upload' button. You can,then, use the next page for uploading videos, creating videos, and also creating videos by compiling your photos.

You may create new videos Online using a photo slide show or video editor. Whatever option you use for creating videos, you would have to fill in its details later. Similarly, if you click on 'Select File to Upload', the upload would start the moment the video file is selected. Once the video upload starts, you should enter details for the concerned video.

- Enter the title of the video like 'Ways to Make Money on YouTube'.
- Enter essential details for the video under 'Description'.
- Enter the tags related to the video.
- You may use any cover photo for a custom thumbnail for your video. The thumbnail lets viewers see a quick snapshot of your video. However, make sure that you do not use an incorrect photo or a photo that is not related to the video.
- You may activate Hindi typing by clicking on 'अ'. You may then enter the title in Hindi.

You have three privacy options for your uploaded video.

1. Public—Any user can view the video under this option.
2. Private—Only you can watch the video.
3. Unlisted—Video can be viewed only by the users who have a link to the same.

If you want to upload to Twitter also, you may select the 'Twitter' option here.

You may also create playlists for your videos. For example, the video 'Ways to Make Money on YouTube' may be in one playlist while another video 'How to Make Money on Website' in another playlist. This helps in segregation and categorising the videos under a head in an organised way.

To customsie settings further, you may click on 'Additional Settings' to get more options. Here, you may disable comments on your video and hide video ratings. You may even visit the 'Monetisation' tab and allow ads in your video to earn income. The 'Publish' button is used once your video is fully uploaded.

Now, income on YouTube only after 10,000 views

For millions of YouTube creators, making videos is not only a creative work but also a source of income. However, as per the new rules, YouTube video creators need 10,000 views on their videos to be able to enable monetisation.

YouTube has also implemented some changes in the 'YouTube Partner Programme (YPP)' that was launched in 2007. Anybody may upload videos to YouTube. If any ad is shown on that video, YouTube shares a part of the related income with the video owner. However, now YouTube would share income with the video owner only after the video gains more than 10,000 views.

YouTube has mentioned in one of its blog posts, "We will not release ads on VPP videos until they hit 10,000 views. This new threshold gives us enough information to determine the validity of a channel. It also allows us to confirm if a channel is following our community guidelines and advertiser policies." After crossing 10,000 views, creators would also receive their share of earnings related to the views up to 10,000.

❑

5

Perfect Name for YouTube Channel

The better the name of a YouTube channel, the easier it is for people to search for that channel and its videos. If you plan to create your own channel, this is the time to choose a good channel name and user name. Choose for your channel a name that targets your genre and highlight your work. The name should also be simple yet catch and something that can be easily remembered. Also, the name should be easy to type to make it convenient for people to search.

Unfortunately, there are millions of users on YouTube and most of them have multiple channels. You need to be a star in the crowd of these channels. If you happen to pick a bad name for your channel, it would be quite difficult for you to attain a top position in that crowd.

If you want to reach the top quickly, you need to pick a top-class name!

How to choose a good name?

Your channel name is the most important component responsible for the success of the channel. Most of you may assume this to be quite trivial, but please be aware that the name of your channel determines its future. There is a strong logic behind the same. If you give a complicated name to your channel, it may create a lot of issues. Do not pick a complicated name. The name should be easy to spell, pronounce and remember. Another point that is quite significant in this respect is to consider what name would represent the genre of your channel.

The benefit of having the right channel name is that a viewer would not forget the same if he finds something interesting on your channel. Instead of searching the topic using keywords, he would come to your channel directly. He may turn out to be your permanent loyal viewer. Many people have made this happen. They have made their channels popular enough to get millions of views on a single video. This kind of success, of course, may be the result of the quality of their work, but their channel names also have a big contribution towards the same.

You should name your channel based its content. For instance, if your channel is related to music, the name should reflect the same. If the channel is cooking-based, the aroma of food should come off its name. If you are creating a sports channel, the name should instantly trigger utterance of words like 'That's another sixer!' That is, as is the work, so should be the name.

If your channel relates to tutorials, its name should have a feeling of a school. Thus, if you are teaching Hindi, the name could be something like 'Hindi Class', 'Hindi Coaching', 'Learn Hindi', 'Hindi Teacher', 'Hindi Class Room', or 'Hindi Pathshala'. The same thing should be done for other fields.

The name should be such that it minimizes the possibility of spelling mistakes while typing. For instance, you should not include numbers in the middle of the channel name. Quite often, people forget those numbers and search with the wrong name. Any spelling issue would create problems for people searching your channel. Hence, it is advisable to avoid numbers amid the name, else it would create search problems. We have seen many good channels getting doomed to failure. The channels have great content but they hardly attract any views just because of the choice of improper names.

Do not use obscene words in the channel name. If you do this, rest assured your channel would die in the womb. You should not copy the name of any other channel or choose a name resembling that of another channel. You should keep in mind that a copy is only an imitation and the original would be unique. If you keep a name resembling an existing one, people would never remember the same. It might also end up benefiting the channel you took name inspiration from.

You should try to ensure that the name that you are going to use is available on other platforms also. This would ensure that your channel has the same name on all domains like Facebook, Twitter, and web domain.

You should pick such a name for your YouTube channel that is everything at once — unique, quirky and precise. The name should be enough to make people interested in watching its videos and subscribing to the channel.

Choose a Creative Name

You have to pick a name that fits your YouTube channel. Hence, before picking the name, decide the genre of the videos that you plan to upload on your channel. If you want to create comedy videos, choose some funny name for your channel to make the it interesting for comedy videos. For instance, if you upload comedy videos on a channel named 'Health Tips', you are sure to fail. It will attract the wrong audience and will also disappoint them. Do not pick a name that is difficult to pronounce and difficult to type for the masses.

Try to Pick a Single-Word Name

Many product-related channels with single-word names are getting quite popular these days, as a single-word name is easier to type and remember as compared to multiple-word names. A single-word name does not mean that you pick up any one word; instead, pick a good name, that has some meaning, and is related to your content.

Combination of Two Words

Try to join two words related to your content. You may create a good name by joining two words. There are many YouTube channels with names created by joining two words. Nobody would get attracted to your YouTube channel if you do not pick a good name for the same. Hence, pick a name that has the potential to attract people.

Define the Objective of Your Channel

Choose a name that defines the purpose of your channel. In order to be a popular YouTuber, you will have to decide what your channel is going to serve and what you are going to provide that nobody else is doing. You might have amusing comedy content, soothing vocals, tasty home-made recipes, DIY gifts, funny comebacks, humorous play writes, thrilling web serials, or anything unique that nobody else has the way you have it. You may pick a name relevant to that very niche.

Pick a name relevant to the content

Your channel name should be relevant to the content of your videos. A contextual name is always more attractive. Your channel name tells your viewers what they are going to find in your channel and its videos. You may attract a great number of viewers just with a unique and contextual name. If you are planning to create health-related videos, you may choose 'Health Tips' as the name of your channel, 'Everyone can dance' for dancing content, 'Study door' for some teaching content and likewise.

Choose a popular word

Choose a popular yet unique name. Consider the preference and popularity among your viewers and select a name that is popular everywhere and can't be forgotten after reading and hearing even once. For instance, if you are launching your channel on the topic of astronomy, you may use words like 'Cosmos' and 'Galaxy'. In this regard, the names 'Marvels' and 'Galaxy' are also good examples.

Choose an easy-to-remember name

Word-of-mouth plays an important role in any kind of success. For your viewers, a complicated name may pose difficulty in remembering and also recommending to others. Choose a name that looks charismatic and is easy to remember; people would be happy to talk about the same.

Stay away from obscenity

Stay away from using derogatory and obscene jokes. YouTube provides freedom of speech but that does not permit you to use improper words and language. Many people use improper language in their videos. Many go to the extent of giving derogatory names to their channels, though the same is wrong and against YouTube's terms and conditions. They are certainly going to have a dark future. By using improper words in your user name and channel name, you are ignoring those who don't like vulgarity. You better avoid words which might be not very community friendly.

Avoid repetition

Many people choose names resembling those of famous channels, thus resulting in their copy-paste replicas. Before making your YouTube channel name official, make sure that there is no existing channel with the same name. You can check this by searching on Google and YouTube. If you find your channel name matching that of any existing channel, you should pick some other name and create a unique identity for yourself.

Pick domain and username free name

If you want your channel to be popular, you need to have a website or blog also. But a still more important point is to check whether the username same as your chosen name is available or not. For instance, if you have picked 'Funny' as your channel name and 'Funny' is not available as a new username, many of your viewers may land on the channel that has the username 'Funny'. Also, even the domain name should be the same as your YouTube channel name, to enable you to create your website and blog for your channel later. This way, you would be able to promote your website through your channel and promote your channel through your website.

Summary

Along with the quality of your videos, it's also important for your channel to have a good relevant name. It is the name which can decide if the user will land onto your channel or not. Hence, pick a name that people would like and that you would be able to share with your friends and acquaintances. Instead of choosing a name resembling that of any existing channel, it would be better to have a unique name. This would create a unique identity for you, just like a person in a white shirt standing among a hundred others in black shirts. After that, you have to become worthy of your channel name. You have to demonstrate your talent as per the name, as it's the talent that works on YouTube and you need to have the same.

Just be unique and the best at what you do!

❑

6

YouTube Channel and Description

You may find millions of videos on YouTube, but out of all those videos, how would you manage to attract more viewers on your video? The answer to this is—the description of your YouTube channel can attract viewers to your videos. And how that can be accomplished—please read on to find out...

You would certainly desire to have the maximum possible subscribers on your YouTube channel and most views on your uploaded videos. And you, definitely, need to be concerned if you are not getting enough views, as it may be due to some problem from your end with your channel.

If your video is not getting views even though the same is of super quality, it may be because you have either not provided any description at all or provided an ineffective description for your YouTube channel. In either case, you are not able to target the right audience for your channel.

Your description provides a viewer with complete information about the content of your channel and videos. You may use this description to convince your visitors to watch your videos. In the absence of any information, they would naturally avoid spending their precious time watching all your videos.

Another point that you need to understand is that when a visitor searches YouTube, the videos that have the right keywords in their channel descriptions are the ones that get listed first.

Suppose you have created a video named ‘How to play cricket?’ Assuming that YouTube has a total of eight videos on the same subject, the YouTube algorithm looks into the quality of all the videos and then other details of the channel like logo, banner, and description. If you are the only one out of all the eight, to have written the description with the right keywords, your video would always rank first in the search result.

As such, there are many other elements that also influence the YouTube algorithm and, hence, the search results.

Choosing the Right Keyword

First of all, you have to choose the right keyword. The right keyword reflects the topic you have used for your channel.

You need to find out the keyword that has been searched the most for the genre of your channel, as the right keyword can help your channel rank at the top in the YouTube algorithm. You may even take the help of keyword research tools to pick the right keyword. For this, Google Ads is a good option as it has Google's own keyword planner and is quite good, besides being free.

Editing Description

Open your YouTube account. Click on 'View Channel'. This will open the main page of your channel. There, you have to click on 'Channel Description'. Once you have completed editing your description, click on 'Done' finally.

Important Tips

- Use only the keywords that are relevant to the content of your channel.
- Don't use the same keywords repeatedly in your YouTube channel description.
- You must use keyword research tools to pick the right keyword.
- The description of the YouTube channel should have at least 200–300 words.
- The description should not be too lengthy.

Writing the description of a video is not a difficult process. You may follow the above steps and write an effective description and make your channel rank on the top.

❑

7

Be a YouTube Earning Wizard

If you also wish to earn as a YouTuber, you may realise your dream by launching your own YouTube channel. Let's see how this dream can be realised and what all things you need to take care of while trying to make money on YouTube.

First of all, launch a channel on YouTube—this is the first step towards making money on YouTube. Link your YouTube account to Google AdSense. YouTube has some policies for the same which you would be required to go through and follow. If you are found eligible, Google would start posting ads in your videos. You may earn a reasonably good income out of the same.

Sponsored Videos

You may even earn income on YouTube using sponsored videos. Under this, you may upload exclusive videos of any company, brand, or shop that is willing to advertise itself to your audience. In simple language, you have to, in a way, promote the company or brand. For instance, if you have a travel-related channel, you may create sponsored videos for a hotel or lodge. This will provide you with an additional source of income other than YouTube earnings. You will have to just make these business companies believe that you have the target audience which can benefit their business. Therefore, sponsored videos are a win-win situation for everyone.

Make money through links

If you are talking about some brand or product in your YouTube video, it would make sense to also provide a link to that product in your description. If any viewer uses that link to buy that product, the company pays you a commission for the same.

Take care of ideas

Millions of videos are getting uploaded on YouTube every single day. Hence, your video needs to be unique to be able to get expected views. Unique ideas and user-friendly content would help you get more views on your videos. You must also ensure that your video quality is good, as people don't like to view low-quality videos or the ones which do not have an audible tone.

Upload videos constantly and consistently

The most important job after creating a channel is to upload videos. If you desire to make money on YouTube, keep uploading at least one or two videos every week. Uploading more videos would ensure a regular increase in total views for your channel. Do keep in mind copyright and media laws while uploading videos.

This is how you get views

Whenever you upload something on your channel, make sure to write a description for that upload. Add relevant tags with the upload.. In the tagging section, enter the keywords that you feel would help your video get listed in search results. This,in fact, is a vital means of getting more views. Hence, add tags as much as possible while performing uploads and use keywords related to the topic.

Make use of every relevant tag and keyword!

Social media

When you launch your YouTube channel, make a note to also create your page on social media like Facebook, Instagram and Twitter. Keep striving to augment 'Likes' for your Facebook page. The 'Likes' on your Facebook page would help get more views. Keep posting links to your YouTube videos on your Facebook page. You may create a video related to questions and reply in Quora posting a link to the same. This would prompt people to view your video. Post stories about the same on Instagram. Promote yourself in the most graceful and desirable manner.

Channel designs should be attractive

Your YouTube channel page is like a mirror that reflects your creativity. There are many layout and design templates on YouTube. You may take their help to create a user-friendly channel.

This is how earning would start

Simply uploading videos on YouTube does not help you make money. You would start making money only after you apply for YouTube's 'Monetisation' programme. For this, you need to go to the monetisation option under the 'Channel' section available on the left side of YouTube.

Prerequisites for monetisation

YouTube has changed the terms and conditions for Monetisation Programme. Now, you can't apply for this programme until you have get a minimum of 10,000 views on your channel. Once this is attained, you may click on 'Monetisation' option and enter your email ID. If everything is according t the guidelines, you would get the approval in around two days.

Monetise every video

Once monetisation approval is received, you need to enable monetisation for every video. For this, you have to just select the 'Edit Video' option and enable monetisation under the 'Monetisation' tab. Just remember, your videos would earn money only after enabling this.

Monetisation may be cancelled

Before approval for monetisation, YouTube checks for any violation of their terms and conditions from your side. Hence, you must ensure to not to upload any copyrighted video to your YouTube channel. If YouTube finds your channel to have any video with copyright belonging to others, it would be difficult for you to get approval.

Save bank details here

After receiving approval, visit the Google AdSense website and update your bank details, address, and other information after logging in with your email ID.

Your first payment

YouTube will send you your first payment only after you have accumulated earnings of at least 100 US dollars from your videos. Once your account shows a balance of 100 US dollars, Google would remit the amount in Indian currency. Before remitting funds, Google sends a PIN to your address. The remittance is made by Google only after the verification of the PIN.

Points to Remember

YouTube is a video platform where you may make money showing your talent. However, please keep in mind that it takes time to start earning there. If you want to make millions, you may get associated with some brands, after hitting a good number of views.

YouTube aims to give everyone a voice and make them a part of the digital world.

YouTube believes that everyone deserves to have a voice and that the world is a better place when we listen, share and build community through our stories.

YouTube core values comprise the following four important freedoms:

1. **Freedom of expression:** YouTube believes that people should get the opportunity to express themselves, raise their voices,, share their views and foster open dialogue. It also maintains that only creative freedom can give shape to fresh voices, perspectives, and possibilities.

2. **Freedom of information:** YouTube believes that everybody should get easy access to information and video is a powerful force for education, building understanding, and documenting world events, big or small.

3. **Freedom of opportunity:** YouTube believes that everybody should get an opportunity to create his own identity, build a business and succeed on his own terms. A majority of people gets to decide what is popular or what is trending without any monopoly or the influence of some limited individuals who are taken into high regard.

4. **Freedom to belong:** YouTube believes that everyone should be able to find communities of support, break down barriers, transcend borders, and connect with people sharing common interests and passions.

YouTube's first video

YouTube platform has almost all the songs and videos that has ever been produced. YouTube is one of the platforms that consume the most Internet. But, are you aware that YouTube took minimal time to reach this point. The point to note is that the first ever video uploaded on YouTube was just 15 years back, on 23 April 2005. The video was uploaded by YouTube co-founder Jawed Karim on 23 April 2005. This video was just 18 seconds long. Jawed's friend Yakov Lapitsky had recorded this video.

This video named 'Me at the zoo' has been viewed more than 60 million times by now. It features Jawed standing in front of elephants in the San Diego zoo and talking about them. Jawed is found commenting on how long is the trunk of the elephant and how it was so cool.

Own product

If you own a product or a business that manufactures or sells, then you may create videos promoting your product for free, thus augmenting your income.

Sell videos

You may even sell all kinds of videos on YouTube. This requires your videos to be of high quality and popular among the audience. You may create videos on any subject and sell the same.

Product review

Review of any product generates maximum earning on YouTube. If your channel has a good number of subscribers and your videos are able to gain significant views, you may get offers from several companies to review their products. They would be happy to offer you the products for free in addition to the fee for reviewing them.

How much you may earn on YouTube?

You may make unlimited money on YouTube. You would be able to earn well if your videos are getting a good number of views. On YouTube, you earn according to the views you get. However, there is no fixed rate for the same. If you get views from countries like USA or UK, you may get good earnings whereas the same number of views from India may fetch you less—around 25 dollars for 100,000 views.

Make more money

You are paid on YouTube according to the number of views. Hence, if you want to make more money on YouTube, you need to get more views on your videos on YouTube. For this, you may share links to your videos on Facebook and Twitter and try to make videos that can go viral and get shared and liked by more and more people.

New features, new earnings

You may augment your earnings on YouTube. Thousands of channels have doubled their income using this feature. YouTube creators may now make more money with their videos. YouTube has released some new features that may help creators to augment their earnings. Let's see what those features are.

Super Chat

Super Chat feature lets fans purchase chat messages during live streaming or premier. There are some 90,000 channels on YouTube that have Super Chat that they use to earn 400 dollars (27,400 rupees approximately) every minute. At present, Super Chat is a good source of income on YouTube. This has helped around 20,000 channels to raise their income up to 65 percent during the last one year.

Super Sticker

Super Sticker feature lets fans purchase animated stickers during live streaming or premier. They use these stickers to convey to their favourite creators how much they love them. These stickers come in different designs, languages, and categories.

Channel membership

Fans may pay 4.99 dollars per month for subscription badges, new emojis, and special features like exclusive live streaming and extra videos. A new feature of membership level has been added to YouTube. This may be used by creators to set up to five levels for membership with different facilities and membership fees.

Merch shelf

Creators may directly sell products, mainly their own merchandise to their fans using the YouTube platform. For this, YouTube has added five new partners that eligible creators may use to sell directly through their channels.

❑

8

Perfect Topic for YouTube Channel

The Internet is being widely used in the present age and many people are working Online to earn income. People have created innumerable websites and YouTube channels and are making millions out of the same. The Internet provides the facility to get all the information sitting in one place and watch contents live or even download them to watch later.

We may use the same Internet prudently to make money. Many people create their YouTube channels but fail to make money. They either don't get enough views on their videos or stop uploading videos very soon, thus preventing their channel to grow.

If you don't upload videos with good content, you may not get subscribers on your YouTube channel. In the present age, it's necessary to create excellent videos and that also with perfect quality. Content and consistency are the two Cs that can help you see your dream of becoming a YouTube start and earning millions come true.

These are some genres that you may use to grow your channel.

Gaming video

If you create and upload gaming videos, your channel may grow quickly with a significant number of views and good subscribers. You need to upload the maximum possible gaming videos for this. If you search gaming videos on YouTube, you may find excellent and popular video gaming channels with a huge number of views and subscribers. As of today, channels are making extremely good gaming videos and gaming video channels are enjoying maximum growth, popularity and the love of their audience

Review

This means unboxing a product and providing all the relevant news in respect of the same. It is basically sharing your own experience with the audience. Today, many people have technical channels offering tech news. You may find many such videos on YouTube and learn how they have been created. You may create a video on any electronic gadget. You may create a video on any gadget coming in the market like mobiles, TVs, and watches. You may provide tech news by creating videos on them. Such channels have moved ahead a lot in the present age. You may also find many such channels on YouTube enjoying a good visitor and subscriber base. Hence, if this is something that interests you, you may also create videos with tech news.

Funny video library

Funny videos relating to kids and animals are quite popular on YouTube. Many people keep looking for such videos for content marketing and you may create a video library for them. You may charge licensing fees from the start-ups who want to use your videos. You may even earn money in the form of commission. Funny videos are being widely watched on Facebook and YouTube these days. Hence, you may create a library of funny videos and use YouTube and Facebook to make the same accessible to people wanting it. You may start earning a good amount of money from the same in a very few days.

Online class

If you are well equipped with the knowledge of anything – some art, some subject, some activity and can teach it well, then you can use these combined tents as well. You don't have to be an expert for the same. It's enough if you can teach just the basics of whatever you personally think you can deliver well.

Online Reality Show

If reality shows can be successful on TV, why not online, then? If you can create reality shows with a fresh and entertaining concept, you would certainly get an audience for the same.

Art and Culture Groups

If you so desire, you may bring together the lovers of any form of art online. Please keep in mind that you can't cover everything under one umbrella and hence, you need to make the right choice. For example, if you want to bring together some music lovers, then you need to get a segregate specification under that as well like Honey Singh Music Lovers, Classical Indian Music, Kishore Kumar Fans, and the list is endless. You will have to pay a lot of attention to the promotion for this. A website will also be required where people may express their views. You may even be required to launch a mobile App. after some time.

School

You may start with a free YouTube channel. YouTube is a good platform for basic learning and people prefer the same.

You can teach anything from music to dance to physics to English to how to eat to literally anything in the world.

Event organiser

Before coming into this business, you need to understand that you will need to decide on your target audience and serve only one group at a time. For example, would you like to start with children or youth? Take care of the convenience of only one group at a time.

Creating cost-effective viral videos

In this business, it all depends on you how many customers you are able to reach and attract. You may initially create videos on your own and if you are successful, you may even take the help of professionals. You may decide your rates depending upon the market rates and some other factors like experience, video length, efforts put in and so on.. If your client provides you with a storyboard, images, and text, you may charge 500 rupees for a 1-minute video. If you are doing all the work on your own, you may charge up to 2,000 rupees and so on

Business model

You may earn money with the help of pay-per-click and pay-per-view advertisements also as per your convenience. Besides this, you may also earn with the help of selling services and related products. If you are planning for long, you may even enter into partnerships with big brands, celebrities, production houses, and TV channels.

Cricket

Indians are famous around the world for their passion for cricket. You may use this passion to your advantage

Cricket also works the same way as the entertainment industry. You may choose your favorite player and open a fan club.

Regional sports club

The craze for IPL would remove all your doubts. You may open an online sports club keeping any specific region in mind and cheering your favourite team.

News and trends

You may create a cricket news channel/updated politics/ current affairs, etc. with the help of the latest news, interesting facts, etc. You may even redirect the audience from Facebook to your channel without spending money on marketing.

Interesting facts

You may collect interesting materials, beyond common knowledge, concerning the topic of your interest, and make them viral by presenting them to your audience.

Politics

Politics has always been a popular domain. If you love to talk and hold discussions on the subject, you have many options. Indian audience spends a good amount of time on Facebook and Twitter to go through political discussions. BJP and Aam Aadmi Party supporters are ubiquitous on the Internet.

Record of government works

You may create influence by creating a record of all the good and bad works of the government. You may present to your audience regular updates on government promises and their actual projects and plans. This would help them analyze whom to vote for in a more critical way.

Presenting news to people

Various kinds of media are already active in the industry and they all present the same news in styles unique to each of them. You may present news in your own style using online media. You may also bring together different channels and political parties on the Online platform and have one on one conversations with them.

Disclosures through an app (mobile or web)

It's quite common to have doubts about the veracity of news available on the Internet due to the unlimited information available there. You may offer an option of a platform for verifying the resource and credibility of the news that is being passed on.

Start-ups and marketing

You may help entrepreneurs in their efforts for starting a new business, marketing, sales promotion, hiring, and project management.

Teach people to sell

Selling products is another major field. If you have experience in sales, you may offer help to others. Sales is truly an art, you can share your techniques and get paid for them.

Design for start-ups

You may even offer services to start-ups as a start-up and network together. You may design their websites and apps and provide services like SEO, SME, Content among many

Hiring and firing

Hiring good people and firing inefficient people—both are quite important aspects. If your observation is clinical and you are able to read people well, you may utilise this talent to help start-ups. To work with human resource and selecting the best potential candidate while replacing the efficient one is quite a skill.

No-cost content marketing

If you are able to help start-ups in learning content marketing, this may be a good option. You may even learn content marketing without spending any money and then work upon it. Once you are comfortable with the subject, you can share your knowledge with others.

Digital marketing (paid + free)

This involves routing traffic to a website through Facebook and Google ads. You may learn this in a few months and then start a digital marketing agency of your own.

Media (news and trends)

You may launch an online media outlet in your favourite domain.

Bollywood news

Though this domain is already quite crowded, but with good contant one can still make way. You may still attract people by publishing movie reviews and entertaining facts connected to celebrities.

Start-up news

You may publish stories about the journey of start-ups and the struggles of their founders. You may even inspire people through their journeys.

Gadget trends

If you are interested in new technologies and gadgets, you may do this job quite efficiently. People are quite interested to learn about new gadgets in simple language and going through their comparisons to know what is the best for them. You may tap and exploit this market. Tech and gadgets are parts of the same domain. You may include both in your channel contents. You may also work on the products of a specific brand.

Fashion trends

This business attracts the youth a lot. You may create a nice platform for fashion trends. People always find this interesting to know what's new in the market. You may be a fashion vlogger as well where you style different clothes and help people choose their outfits.

Stock market and business news

Stock market and business-related news is valuable for people and you may get good traffic for the same. Be careful in choosing the news items. This is a complex subject and people would love to understand the same in simple language. You may help them in this regard. For this, you should be very well versed with what you are talking about.

Technology and software

It's not a difficult job for software engineers to start a business in the tech industry. If you are short of ideas, you may get a clue from the example of the Stack Overflow community. You may pick any such topic as 3-D Printing, Android, or Arduino.

Tech start-up

Ideas are abundant in this domain. You don't need to hire professionals right from the first day. You may even join as a co-founder for technical development. If you are good in sales/marketing, you may even learn things by yourself.

Mobile app

If you have even a little bit of experience in the development of mobile apps, you may try the same. This is in high demand in the today's digital space.

Online community

Communities would be always a dependable source of information for real users. Reddit, Stack Overflow, and Zomato are typical examples.

Financial products

Products like insurance, mutual funds, and home loans may even be sold online. Banks are ready to pay commission for the same. You may even create a product comparison website to help people compare products and pick the best matching their requirements. You may even sell the mentioned financial products to them online along with this service. You may also charge for giving recommendations of buying the financial products suiting them the best.

Website for Filing IT Returns

Very few people are aware of how the processes relating to Income Tax (IT) work. Most people don't know how to file their IT returns. You may be of help to them in this regard. You may charge for filing their returns.

Finance

If you are good at finance, YouTube and Internet have plenty of options for you. Newspapers generally use standard language to present finance-related information and many of the complexities are not explained properly. You may use your blog or YouTube channel to do the same. You may explain complex finance topics in an easier and simpler way.

Consultation on Finance Matters

Where to invest funds, how much to spend, where to save, how to save tax, and how to do retirement planning—these are some of the issues that common people generally lack the knowledge to find a solution for. You may be of help to them as a financial expert.

Selling subscription-based premium content

The content or information available for free on the Internet may be incorrect and misleading too. In order to resolve this issue, some authors create content based on their reliable research and charge fees for the same. You may sell your research reports or e-books on financial products for 50 to 1,000 rupees. Jagoinvestor and Capitalmind work on the same business model.

Finance matters

People interested in discussing finance matters in-depth, far beyond the common topics like retirement and investment, may be brought together on a single platform. People can have a platform to share their views and deep financial knowledge and analyse all of the information put on the table accordingly.

Comedy videos

Comedy videos get a good number of views these days. This can be observed on YouTube where you may find plenty of comedy videos. Hence, you may also create a channel for comedy videos; they are considered to be quite popular and they are also usually very short, running for 2–4 minutes. You may create them on your mobile also. This is a simple job and if you create comedy videos for children, they may get you a much better count of views and subscribers. This would be quite rewarding for your channel. For youth, you can also set up a start up background and do the same.

Product video

A product video may be made on any market product; e.g., new T-shirt, pants, mobile, bag, laptop, washing machine, etc. You may create a video to provide information on any product that you buy in the market. These are also very good videos for your channel. They may fetch you a good number of views, as in the present age, people do not prefer to go out and explore products. They would be happy to watch videos Online. Thus, if you post such videos, it would be helpful to them and beneficial for your channel also. This is credible content and also informative for the audience.

How-to

'How-to' refers to a detailed explanation of the pros and cons of any product. You may create videos on such topics. For instance, if you purchase a new mobile, you may talk about its strong points. These are generally popular videos and they get significant views these days. Cooking and baking videos are also quite popular under this type.

Prank video

These videos are just like funny videos but they are also a bit different from them. These videos include content on how to hurt or tease or prank somebody. You can find plenty of such videos on YouTube. You may go-through them to understand how they have been made. You may also create such videos and upload them to your channel. This would boost views on your channel. These videos are quirky and entertaining.

Education news

You must be aware of education news. Education news is based on information related to education. If you love academic work, you may share your knowledge through videos.

Beauty tips

You may create videos on beauty tips, but you must have proper knowledge of the same. Beauty and hairstyle-related videos get a good number of viewers these days. Skincare routines are also very popular under this category.

Related to plants, trees, and environment

Of late, curiosity about plants, trees, and the environment has grown considerably among people. You may take advantage of the same and create videos providing information related to plants that can be grown in flowerpots at home. Bonsai-related videos also would be useful.

Help in Accounting

You don't need to be a chartered accountant or legal financial adviser to provide help in accounting. It's enough to have a degree in finance or commerce. You may have basic knowledge of software like tally and you are good to go.

Help in Preparing for Finance-Related Examinations

There is a dearth of quality videos on finance-related topics. You may fill this gap. You may share your knowledge to help commerce and finance students do well in their examinations.

Health

This domain is quite sensitive. Consider working in this field only if you have a good grasp of related knowledge.

Precise Review of Doctors

People, most of the time, find it difficult to choose a good doctor. In the circumstances, a review may come handy for them. If you are able to get your viewers discount in fees for major treatments, it could be an extremely helpful initiative. Other initiatives could be providing a helping hand to the poor for their medical treatments and creating communities for providing support to patients.

Create a community for support to patients with depression

People generally hesitate to share these kinds of problems and you may provide the option of an online platform to bring them together. You may even provide the right guidance for the treatment of the sufferers. The art of effective listening is very important for this initiative.

Fashion and beauty

Women spend a good amount of money on their fashion and beauty products. If you also have an interest in fashion, you may launch an online business. You may also refer to which products should be used for the specific skin types.

Styling ideas

After research, you may find what kind of outfits people are currently looking for, for events like parties, weddings, etc. This is a very dynamic field requiring you to be always updated on the trends.

Ideal locations for buying fashion products

You may offer suggestions for ideal locations for budget shopping and premium shopping.

Home remedies for baby care

Make sure to do proper research before suggesting any home remedy, especially for babies.

Tour and travel

Today, travel has become such a pursuit that people are always ready to spend lavishly for the same. They are always on the lookout for new and exciting places. There also exists a large category of people who prefer budget traveling. You may provide an attractive online platform to these amateurs. You may become a travel vlogger.

Event management

You may launch an event management service by creating a page on Facebook or YouTube. You may cover different kinds of events, weddings being one of them. Additionally, you may do business by providing information regarding any specific planning according to different budgets.

In addition to the above, there is an abundance of topics for you to choose from. Some of them being information relating to science and languages, biographies, nature, magic, song and music, poetry, health, pollution, obesity, and how things are made. This list is non exhaustive.

❑

9

Video Content and Quality

Strive to keep the content of your videos superior. Never try to copy and paste any kind of video or image from other videos or websites as this would make your video rank low in search results and also lead to some copyright issues. It might also result in a low view count for your videos and,hence, low earnings for you.

Audio-video quality

Use phones having high-quality cameras and high-grade audio recording features to capture your video. This would ensure that your content has good-quality audio and video and whatever you are presenting therein can be clearly viewed and heard. If your video has low-quality audio, the listener would not be able to clearly understand what you are trying to convey. Similarly, if the video quality is poor, the viewer would not be able to clearly see what you are trying to present and he would not be able to appreciate your content.

This would adversely impact the image of your channel and the viewer would not return to watch your videos, thus lowering your view count.

Keywords

Do conduct thorough research for keywords related to the topic that you are going to use in your video. The title of your video should reflect the topic on which the same is created. If you don't do that, viewers would have a problem searching for your video and they would not be able to watch the video that they want. Therefore, use keywords but make sure they are right and relevant.

Add thumbnails

Add thumbnails to your videos. Your thumbnail should be related to the topic that you have used for your video. This would help viewers get to know the topic of the content of your video. If a viewer finds on your video the same banner that he is looking for, he would be quick to open your video. You should share your videos on Facebook, Twitter, WhatsApp, etc., to augment your earnings. Also, make sure that the thumbnail is not misleading and actually highlights what is in the video.

Ensure precise editing

Don't upload your video to your channel immediately after creating the same. Many a time, minor errors and omissions get overlooked and the video gets uploaded with them. For instance, you might have missed some information that you wanted to convey in your video. Hence, make sure to edit your video meticulously and upload the same on your channel only after reviewing that multiple times. This would help the viewer understand the video content well and get thorough information on the topic he is looking for. If he is content with the value your content added to him, he would be compelled to revisit your channel.

Create playlists

If you are creating a video series on a topic, e.g., a tutorial on any subject, you should use a playlist for the same. This would help a visitor to your channel view all related videos on the subject easily. Playlists are very effective and help viewers to easily navigate through a channel.

YouTube channel: Precautions

Many people create YouTube channels and then make several mistakes, resulting in their channels being frozen or worse, deleted.. Hence, you should follow YouTube guidelines to avoid any kind of issues in the future.

- Don't download some other person's video and upload it on your YouTube channel. This is a violation of copyright and is a crime plus unethical.
- Avoid uploading any video with nudity or sexual content.
- Don't create a video that has contents offensive to any religion or community.
- Your channel may run the risk of getting deleted if YouTube community guidelines are not followed.

Views

Earnings on YouTube are made from the videos that are viewed by a large number of people. Take care to ensure superior quality for your videos. Don't forget to write a description for your videos and add relevant tags to them. Use keywords used in video searches for those tags.

❑

10

Earning Faces on YouTube Channels

Digital media, besides being a means of self-branding, is also a major source of income. The YouTube platform of social media has not only turned many talents into superstars but also showed them a way to make good earnings. In the same context, seven-year-old Ryan is the youngest popular star on YouTube.

Seven-year-old Ryan ranks first in the list of top 10 highest paid YouTubers as per Forbes magazine. Ryan, who reviews toys on YouTube, made 22 million US dollars just in the single year 2018. Ryan has left even 21-year-old Jake Paul behind to take the first rank in respect of earnings on YouTube. There are around 25.1 million clients on his channel. Ryan has made more money even in comparison to makeup artist Jeffree Star and Swedish gamer Felix Kjellberg. Ryan has more than 25.1 million followers on YouTube.

Ryan, an American, has a channel on YouTube, named 'Ryan Toys Review'. Ryan reviews toys on the same. Every video on the channel gets millions of views and many millions of comments. His family runs this channel on YouTube and Ryan reviews toys on the same. During the initial days of the channel, he was just seen playing with the toys, but as the videos started getting popular, he started delivering reviews also for the same toys.

Ryan's mother says, "Looking at kids on other YouTube channels, he also one day expressed his desire to be on a channel. We then took him to a shop to buy his first toy—I think it was a Lego train set. This was the start of Ryan's journey." Ryan's mother quit her job after finding him engrossed in YouTube and after looking at the earnings being made out of the same. Now she devotes her entire time to Ryan on YouTube. Most of the viewers on Ryan's channel on YouTube are kids aged between three and seven years. The majority of his followers are from the USA. He also has a large number of viewers from Britain and the Philippines. His latest toy Mini Mogul and other toys are available in Walmart stores.

Five guys combined 'Sports Crew'

Five guys' combined 'Sports Crew' is currently overwhelming YouTube. Kobi, Caury Kapas, Getet Hilbert, Cody Jones and

Tylor Tony are prominent among them. They have around 175 million followers. This sports crew is known for its complicated moves. Each of them is an expert in his shots. They are experts in triggering Dominos-falls of Joe Oros while tossing ping-pong balls.

Series on Disney

Ireland resident Jon McLaughlin is also quite popular on YouTube. People love his commentary on colourful video games. He has released a new series for Disney.

Felix Kjellberg

Swedish Felix Kjellberg is a big player on YouTube. His well-known programme 'Scandal' has almost 72.5 million followers. However, his programme was removed by Google because of some issue with one video. His advertisers were still not disappointed. They did not part ways with Scandal. He is earning millions out of the same.

Logan Paul

Google had removed a favourite programme of 23-year-old Paul from YouTube in January 2018. Paul had uploaded to YouTube a video of a suicide committed in Japan. This suicide was committed by hanging from a tree. The filming of this video in Japan resulted in the removal of all advertisements on Paul's popular channel. Paul tendered an apology to Google for the same. Despite all this, loyal followers of Paul continued with their thriving business.

Bhuvan Bam

Bhuvan is quite popular on YouTube. His comedy videos based on generic stories are immensely popular among people. Bhuvan plays 5–6 roles at the same time in his videos. He plays all the roles of parents, friends, and relatives by himself. The salient feature of his videos is that they are shot on his own phone. Delhi resident Bhuvan is also a professional musician and makes good money from his live shows and concerts. His YouTube channel is one of the fastest-growing channels on the platform. Bhuvan's YouTube channel has 17.6 million subscribers.

Sandeep Maheshwari

Sandeep Maheshwari is a motivational speaker and also one of the fast-emerging entrepreneurs of India. He is primarily known for his unique speaking style. He conducts seminars to inspire those youth who are scared of public speaking and have lack self-confidence. He is now quite popular on YouTube. Capable of prompting people to change their perspective on life, Sandeep owns a YouTube channel with around 14.8 million subscribers.

Nisha Madhulika

For those trying to learn cooking, Nisha Madhulika is not a new name. People go to her channel to find the recipe for any new dish. Nisha launched her cooking blog in 2007. Later, she started her YouTube channel at the age of 52. Initially, her husband would help her in technical jobs. She now has a team of her own to create and refine content. Her channel is among the most popular cooking channels on YouTube. There are around 9.21 million subscribers on Nisha Madhulika's cooking channel.

Sanam Puri

Sanam Puri is the lead singer of the 'Sanam' band. This band creates remixes for old hit songs with new music for his music-loving followers. There are four artists in this band; they all play different instruments. This channel is quite popular on YouTube. It has 7.38 million subscribers.

Technical Guruji

Gaurav Chaudhary's 'Technical Guruji' is a technical channel on YouTube. Different kinds of gadgets including mobile phones and TVs are reviewed on the same. Gaurav creates his videos in both Hindi and English to reach the maximum number of people. His product reviews are not only informative but also reliable. He even arranges tech talks to make his viewers conversant with technology. He has 16.7 million subscribers.

Shruti Arjun Anand

Shruti had started her YouTube channel by posting weekly skincare tips and beauty products. It was her collection of excellent videos on makeup and hair care that made her a perfect beauty YouTuber. Her videos cover styling tips, makeup reviews, and reviews of beauty products. Some 7.18 million people have subscribed to her channel.

Varun Pruthi

Varun Pruthi runs a YouTube channel named 'ActorVarunPruthi'. Varun is a social worker. He creates videos on social issues and helps poor and deprived people. He even buys items made by the poor. His channel has 4.11 million subscribers.

Kanan Gill

Kanan is one of the famous stand-up comedians in India. He knows how to bring a smile to the faces of his audience. He has become famous by presenting reviews of Bollywood films in a humorous style. A software engineer by profession, Kanan quit his job and took up comedy as his full-time career. He has been quite successful in the same.

❑

11

Farmers Earning Millions on YouTube

Everybody in the country is aware of the issues of rising inflation and unemployment. Many agriculturists are quitting farming because of rising costs and inadequate earnings. This has resulted in a situation where even the youth in villages have started considering farming as a losing proposition and migrating to cities in search of a better income. However, we are going to tell you about some of the farmers who have worked for breaking this perception. They are not only making good money out of farming but also sharing the tips for the same with others.

Yash Jat

Yash Jat needs no introduction today. He operates a YouTube channel in the name of 'My Kisan Dost'. He has taken up this as his full-time job. Before coming on YouTube in 2015, he used to write blogs on crops. People, then, suggested him to create videos to be able to reach more and more people. His channel has 675,000 subscribers today. He never expected so many people would connect with him on YouTube. In his videos, he covers agriculture-related news, new farming techniques, animal husbandry, floriculture, and crop-related advice. His current focus is on Aloe Vera.

Darshan Singh

Darshan Singh was born in a family of farmers. He has done M.A. in Political Science. He is now operating his YouTube channel 'Farming Leader' as his full-time job. He has been posting farming-related videos right from 2017. Gradually, his videos started getting more views. By now, more than 2 million people have subscribed to his channel. The videos he posts mostly provide suggestions for the farmers to raise their income. Awareness among people is growing and farming-related videos are in good demand these days.

Ayyappan

Ayyappan is a software engineer was born in a family of farmers. He got farming tips from his father and launched his YouTube channel. He regularly posts videos covering problems related to farming. He is making good money on YouTube. His YouTube channel 'Come to Village' has more than 800,000 subscribers. He focuses more on tractor-related issues.

❑

Addendum

Other Sources for Online Income

With the advent of the World Wide Web, every Internet user is having a question in his mind, can he use this vast international network for making money? Who would not like to earn some extra income (that also possibly without investing time or labour)? There is an abundance of advertisements in newspapers calling people to 'make money on the Internet without doing anything.

If you look at the Internet as an additional source of income and if you possess any talent or if you are ready to invest your time and effort , you would certainly find people ready to appreciate your services or expertise somewhere in this ocean of the Internet. In any case, all the people connected with the Internet have the same needs. If an American citizen gets his requirement serviced by an Indian for a relatively cheaper cost, why would he have any objection to the same? Yes, it is possible to earn extra money on the Internet in a perfectly legal way provided you are ready to offer some outstanding product, service, talent, or expertise. If you are conversant with the modalities of Internet marketing, then, that would be the icing on the cake!

FREELANCING

Freelancing means to work independently for somebody else without being formally employed by that person or company. While people who are already employed use their spare time to take up such assignments, there is also no dearth of people who have made freelancing the means of their primary livelihood. The Internet is replete with freelance projects right from web designing to writing, graphic designing, page designing, programming, copywriting, TV programme scripting, sales and marketing, finance and share trading, legal consultancy services, engineering, and manufacturing. Usually, such assignments are available as projects and a fixed sum is paid for every project. While companies find this convenient to get their work done at good rates and with better timelines, the freelancers get an opportunity to make extra money using their spare time without quitting their existing jobs, with the experience of new assignments coming as an additional benefit.

There are many sites available for people interested in freelancing; they may start taking assignments after registration on those sites. Most of the freelancing sites assign projects based on bidding. The lower your bid, the better would be your chances to get the project.; Though quality of work, seniority of the concerned person, reputation and experience of other customers are also given due consideration. The website takes a small fee in lieu of the project assigned to you. Some websites even charge a fee for their membership. Some of those sites for freelancers are—elance, Freelancer, Rent A Coder, and Logoworks.

Translation, Editing, Proofreading

Though this may be treated as a kind of freelancing project, this is, of late, being considered to be an independent category based on the gradual increase in this type of job on the Internet. Many of the websites work as a platform to connect the companies seeking such jobs and translators and editors providing or outsourcing such services. They help many good translators residing in small towns to be able to secure translation projects that they could not have secured in the absence of the Internet. If you have a good mastery of any two languages, you can also try this option for additional income.

Language is also one of the strengths of Indians. As a country, we have several languages used by different people. Most of the assignments that are available on the Internet are in English. Speaking English is effortless in South India, but North Indians have to make an effort for the same. As a result, many of the articles, press releases, or books may need to be translated. Both kinds of jobs—translation from English to Indian languages and vice versa—may be done. The market other than English has jobs in languages like Spanish, French, Arab, and German.

Thanks to globalisation, the number and need of documents to be translated from one language to another are constantly growing and this is going to continue for a long time. On these websites, the translators are generally paid a specific remuneration per word depending on the quality of work. Many a time, the client demands the translation in a specific format and hence, the translators conversant with different software formats are able to earn better than others. Some of the well-known websites providing opportunities for translation jobs on the Internet are ProZ, TranslatorsCafe, Trailly, TRADUguide, LangJobs, Transquotation, and Elance.

Photography

If you feel you have a talent for photography, you should be aware that photographs for websites, presentations, brochures, papers and magazines, newspapers, etc., are always in demand. There are some stock photography websites available on the Internet; they maintain stock of high-quality photographs and graphics in millions. Publishing houses and website creators may buy photographs of their choice from them. However, many a time, these websites do not have photographs matching the requirements of the customers. For instance, if somebody is looking for a photograph of the ancient wrestling style of Kerala, he would hardly find the same on a stock photography website. Similarly, photographs relating to some small village, any specific incident, or a forgotten individual are many a time difficult to find. If you have such photographs, you may sell the same to stock photography websites. Thanks to an increasing number of websites, there is high global demand for photographs of even common objects like a spoon, a bowl, a door, a lamp, a pen, an ink, a computer, clouds, trees, a terrace, and sports. You may click good-quality photographs of things around you and send them to these websites.

Some government organisations like US Naval Institute and travel websites like Outtravel are also always looking for such photographs. If you so wish, you may even develop your own website and create your portfolio of high-quality photographs. While sending photographs to these websites, please do make sure that your photographs are not violating any trademark, copyright, or the law. Some of the sites that buy photographs are iStockphoto, Shutterstock, Dreamstime, Adobe, and Pond5.

HR SERVICES

You might have heard some companies pay incentives to their employees who help in the recruitment of new employees as per their requirements. Some companies pay similar incentives to common Internet surfers, who refer to them some suitable potential candidates. This amount may be anywhere from 50–1000 dollars provided the candidate is selected for recruitment. The interesting fact is that if you are successful in getting even one candidate recruited by an employer during a month, your objective of additional income gets fulfilled. What is required is to keep looking for good candidates everywhere right from job posting websites to various forums, social networking sites, and your group of friends. In this kind of work, people who are able to effectively coordinate between recruiters and candidates tend to be more successful. Companies like HireMagic pay incentives to them also. Some of the useful sites in this field that pay incentives to people referring good candidates are Referearns, Joinin, Who-Do-You-Know-For-Duff, Bohire, and Wisestep.

SELF-PUBLISHED BOOK

If you love writing, you would be happy to know that many sites provide options to write books Online for payment and even to earn through their royalties. One of these sites 'Amazon' has a feature known as Kindle Direct Publishing. Under this, anybody may write a book Online and place the same on Kindle Store. The writer may get up to 70 percent of royalty on the sale of such a book. You may even become a regular member at the site by opening your account. Besides that, Kobo, Draft2Digital, and Smashwords are also good self-publishing platforms.

Google AdSense

You may even make some money by placing ads on your blog through Google AdSense. Just allow ads provided by Google AdSense to be displayed on your blog. This will pay you for every click made on an ad displayed on your blog. Google AdSense provides various kinds of ads like videos, images, texts, and banners. You need to select the best out of the same and place the same on your blog.

Buy-sell ad

This also is a way of online marketing. Ads may be sold directly through this. They charge a commission in lieu of the ads provided to your blog. You don't have to make direct contact with these advertisers.

Paid review

Writing reviews for software or other products can also earn you a fair amount. If you have a good command of writing, you may make money through this. Besides this, Infolinks is also an option.

Earning by selling old items

This is an easy option to make money Online. Under this, you may earn by selling old items lying in your house Online. Many of the websites offer the facility to place ads free of cost for such useless items. Thus, you may sell old items by uploading their photographs on sites like OLX, Quikr, and Craiglist.

Virtual call centre agent

You may even work from home as a call centre agent. Liveops provides you with such an option. You may visit this site and become a company agent. On its home page, apply to become an agent. This would require a phone, a computer, and an Internet facility at home. You need to have a good command of English to be able to talk to the clients directly and sell them products. Even if you are not good in English, you may take up this work as, immediately, after a call is connected, the company would tell you what is to be spoken, i.e., immediately after the call starts, you would get on your screen all details that you have to speak. You may earn around 7 to 15 dollars per hour through this website.

Swagbox.com

Swagbox.com is a famous website where you may register for free and start earning. You may connect to the same through Facebook also. You may be earning less money here but you would get many items that are of use in your daily life like mobiles, hard disks, mugs, and T-shirts. You have to just spend some time on this website for shopping, searching, playing, chatting, and collecting information on products. In return, the website would award some points to you. You may either use these points for shopping or convert them into cash.

Virtual assistant

Virtual assistants work on the Internet from home and can manage the business across the world. Anybody who knows how to respond to an email, how to create business documents like PowerPoint presentations and Excel sheets and how to manage blogs and websites can be a virtual assistant.

Medical transcript

The medical transcript is the best work from home activity. Under this, a person sitting thousands of miles away transcripts recorded medical dictation of a doctor. This requires a computer, a fast Internet connection, and earphones. If possible, go through a course on the medical transcript. Websites like Guru.com and Freelancer.com offer freelance works of medical transcription. Besides the above, there are Online medical transcript companies that offer similar assignments.

Web developer

There are only a few web developers who are masters in their field. Such people are able to earn ₹ 150,000 to ₹ 200,000 per month through freelancing. They need to have good knowledge of coding and website designing. Freelancer.com may help you in this regard.

Apps business

Millions of applications are getting created and sold for smartphones and tablets. If you have a good idea for an app, you may even get the same developed by some developer. Once the app is ready, you may register the same on Google, Apple, and Windows Store of Microsoft.

Travel agent

This involves activities right from planning a tour to booking flights, rail tickets, bus tickets, hotels, etc. There are many Online travel companies in India. In order to be a travel agent, you must have a website of your own. Thus, if somebody is planning a trip to Goa or any other place and trying to search for an online travel agent, your website should appear in their search results amid the top recommendations.

Data entry

Data entry is the cheapest way of earning Online. If you have basic computer knowledge and typing skills, there are plenty of opportunities for you to make money in this field. You may take help from Freelancer or Simply Hired in this regard.

Own website

Developing a website is not a difficult job now. You may pay and get this done by somebody or make some effort to do the same by yourself. If you sell something to your visitors and your website attracts visitors regularly, you may earn through Google AdSense. The more the number of your visitors, the more would be your earning.

Affiliate marketing

If your website has been successful, you may place your web links on the websites of other companies. If any visitor uses the link provided in your channel to buy a product, you may get some money. Affiliate programme promotes products of websites like Flipkart, Amazon, Snapdeal, and eBay. This has become the hottest online job in India, as this is a fast-growing sector in the country. You may become Flipkart, Amazon, Snapdeal, or eBay affiliates and earn 4 to 10 percent commission on each sale.

Virtual assistantship (Manage work online)

Suppose a gentleman is a high-profile person. He does not have time to manage online activities. In that case, he would hire a virtual assistant. This would not require the assistant to physically be with the client. He may work from anywhere through the Internet. You may work as an employee for somebody or even set up your own business.

Online tuition (Online masterji)

If you are an expert in a subject, it may be a great thing as, with such a large population in the world, there is surely somebody somewhere looking for the knowledge that you possess. You may start sharing your knowledge on the Internet. You may be probably doing good to a student appearing in a board examination or may be helping somebody who is lost somewhere to return home. If you share knowledge on a proper website, you may earn also. YouTube is really a good place for the same.

In Western countries, parents don't have time to help their children complete their homework. Over and above that, the problem of finding a good and affordable tutor is equally tedious. The Internet has come as a boon to such parents. They are able to arrange Online tuition for their children from foreign teachers at comparatively cheaper rates, thus helping both parties. The availability of competent teachers of English, mathematics, and science has already established India as a preferred destination in the field of Online tuition. If you are also a teacher or have good command over any subject, you may offer tuition to domestic and foreign students while sitting at home. If you are able to secure more than one foreign student, your income may even be better than your full-time job.

Several website use latest Internet-based technologies for online tuition and teachers are trained on the same before they take up assignments. Besides tuition for any specific subject, opportunities even exist for helping students complete their projects and for coaching them for various entrance examinations. Tutors are paid anywhere between 5–25 dollars per hour for the same. What's wrong in making that much money by just working for one hour, that also from your own home? But, how to find such students? Answer to that also is available on the Internet itself. Some of such sites are TutorVista, Transtutors, OnlineTuition, BuddySchool and HomeTutors network. Tuition is a website to which around 77,000 students and 22,000 teachers across the world are connected.

Earn by reading ads

There are many websites where you may sign up and even earn by reading ads. After signing up, you will have to login to those sites on a regular basis and click on the ads being displayed on the dashboard of your account. Most of such sites would also send you ads through SMS and even pay for reading them. By spending only 10–20 minutes on the computer every day, you may be able to earn more than that you earn by attending office.

Online micro jobs

Micro jobs simply means minor tasks that may need just seconds to complete. There are dozens of sites like MTurk and Microworkers where you may earn between 5–100 rupees by completing a task.

Blogging

Blogging is one of the best jobs on the Internet. You may create a simple blog and promote the same by posting some good content. You may create both free and paid blogs. You may earn from your blog by placing ads on Ad Network. This works quite like Google AdSense and you earn out of every click made on the ads appearing on your blog. Blogging is an effective means of earning. You may choose any favourite subject for blogging. If your views are appreciated by people, the number of visitors on your blog may see a gradual increase. Once your blog becomes popular and the same starts getting a good number of visitors, you may earn good money by placing ads of products of different companies on your blog. This earning may run into thousands or even millions. There are many sites on the Internet that offer to create blogs for free. You may pick a template of your choice for the same. It's easy to create a blog, but running a good blog requires you to be conversant with blogging techniques.

Online writing job

This is a job for people who love writing. Online writing jobs are popular as every website on the Internet needs the content to be updated regularly. You may earn anywhere between 250–1000 rupees from this job.

Buy-sell domains

If you are looking for a good income, this is the job for you. You may buy domains at cheap rates on GoDaddy or any other domain registrar and then sell the same at higher prices to those looking for those domain names. Here, you need to do proper research and find out good domain names. After some time, you may invite bids for those domain names.

Online sale

Many people are making millions by selling their products on major shopping sites like eBay, Amazon, and Flipkart. You just need a good product. You may then sign up on any such site, list your product with the price, and start selling. You don't need to talk to anybody. You will receive an order through the mailbox and you just need to deliver the product ordered through a courier company.

Online survey, research, review

In Online surveys, some companies ask you a few questions related to some products or anything else. You have to just answer them—either 'yes' or 'no' or something specific—and submit them Online. You may get survey tasks on daily basis and you need to complete them which will enable some earnings.

Many websites pay for completing Online surveys, conducting research, and writing product reviews. Once the work is done, payment is credited to your account. Here you need to be cautious. You share your bank details with them. Hence, you should go ahead only after verifying the reputation of the website. Many a time, those providing the tasks usurp some of the payments.

Websites normally transfer payments directly into your account. You have to just create your account using your email ID and start filling out surveys. There are some survey sites like ClixSense, NeoBux, Global Test Market, SwagBox, StarPanel, and IndiaSpeaks that make good payments. Do make sure to go through reviews before joining any such site, as the genuineness of the sites may be found in reviews only. You should go through at least 10 reviews.

Earning from Captcha

Whenever you create an account or login on to a website, you are asked to fill out a captcha. Similarly, some websites get captchas created against payment. You have to just open your account on that website and start working. Websites like CaptchaTypers, ProTypers, Captcha2Cash, and 2Captcha offer jobs for creating captchas.

Earning from mobile phone

Google Play Store has many Apps that you may use to make money. You just need to download those Apps and start working. Some such Apps are Ibotta, Spokk, MakeMoney, and CashPirate. You may easily start earning with all these Apps.

Earning from the sale of paintings

If you are a good painter, you may earn money on the Internet by selling your paintings. For this, you may create quality designs for coffee cups, T-shirts, bags, etc., and post them on a website for sale. For this, there are some websites like Jaisal.com where you may sell your designs.

Earn by Providing Technical Services

If you are a technical expert and wish to use your expertise for making money, the Internet may prove to be a blessing for you. Some websites like oDesk and Elance provide such opportunities by helping you to connect with people who need your technical services. Thus, you may earn by providing technical services over the Internet.

Earn by Selling Music

If music is your hobby and you have good knowledge of the same, you may compose music and sell the same on the Internet. Some websites like Amazon and Google Play provide such opportunities. Your music may be bought for songs, advertisements, and ringtones and you may get paid well for the same.

Earn by Designing Themes

If you know a coding language, you may make millions by designing fresh and high-quality themes for blogs. You may sell your best themes on your own blog and even on other theme stores. Many bloggers keep looking for fresh designs for their blogs. You may earn a good income by creating theme designs.

Earn through Facebook

Facebook is the most popular social networking site in the world. It's an excellent platform to connect with friends, relatives, and new people. As we already know, many millions of people are already connected on Facebook. You may create your Facebook page and Facebook groups and use the same to make money by sharing your own or others' websites or products. No investment is required to earn on Facebook. Nothing is to be paid for creating an account, page, or group there. Sometime back, Facebook has introduced an option to buy and sell in groups; that can be used to buy and sell any products—it may be from your business or shop or it may even be already used.

Creating a Facebook page is quite important for any blog, business, celebrity, or even a brand. Those already having a Facebook account may quite easily create a Facebook page. Create a page on a topic that may attract maximum likes for you. If your page gets a good number of likes, you may make money through that page.

As such, this is correct that Facebook does not pay you anything directly. You will have to use some methods or magical cure for the same. You must already be having a Facebook account. What you have to do is to connect more and more people to your account or your Facebook page.

The more the number of people on your friends' list, the more would be your earnings.

Earn through Amazon.com

Amazon.com is the largest e-commerce website in the world. Millions of people shop on the site every day. If you use your brains well, you may make millions on Amazon.com. The process is quite simple. You need to create an affiliate account on the site. Once the affiliate account is opened, you will receive the affiliate link that you can share with your friends, your relatives, or anybody else. And when somebody uses that affiliate link to buy anything on Amazon.com, you will receive a specific commission. You may find out from Amazon.com what would be the rate of your commission. You don't have to pay any amount for creating an affiliate account on Amazon.com. This service is totally free.

Fever

Fever also is an excellent old website for Online earning. People make good money here. You have to first create your account on Fever; this is entirely free. Many people visit this site looking for somebody to get their work done. If you know that job, you may find great opportunities for earning here. As you go on helping more and more people and completing their jobs, the number of your clients would go up. You need to have a very professional account here. You will have to provide all the details in order to attract more clients. Another point that you need to keep in mind for improving your earnings here is that you must serve your clients professionally—completing their jobs meticulously and delivering the same on time.

oDesk

oDesk is a good website for making money Online. You will get more earning opportunities here as there is no limit on jobs and payments on this website. You may charge at your will on oDesk. People are easily making millions on this website and the great thing is that this is a very old and reputed website. Payments for completed jobs are made on time. You will have to create an Online account here and make your profile professional.

Earning by Reading Emails

Email marketing has a lot of importance in the virtual world. You may be using different mail services every day, but have you ever thought that you may even earn by reading emails?

Send Earnings—You may earn money on this website through emails, surveys, and Online shopping. You will have to first open your account and get your registration confirmed. You are paid 1 dollar for reading one email here.

If you don't visit this site for continuous six months, your account may get deactivated. You must have a balance of at least 30 dollars (approximately 2,500 rupees) in your account while requesting requesting payment.

Matrixmails—This website is a better option for earning through emails. This website is operational since 2002. On this website, while reading emails, visit sites using offers and share details with others to earn money. Somewhere between 25–50 dollars may be earned every hour here.

Cash4Offers—You may make money using this website also. Once you become a Gold member of the website, your receive payments in less than 72 hours. You may here earn by reading emails, completing surveys, using cash offers, playing online games, and getting accounts opened for your friends. You get around 5 dollars immediately after you sign-in on the website.

PaisaLive—If you wish to earn money quickly without making any investment, this is the website that provides you with options. You will receive 99 rupees immediately after opening your account at PaisaLive. You will also receive 10 rupees on getting your 10 friends to open their accounts here. After the first 10 friends, you will receive 2 rupees for every additional friend. You receive anywhere between 25 paise to 5 rupees for reading emails. The website makes payment through cheques once in 15 days.

Money Mail—On this website, you may earn by sparing your 15 minutes a day for reading emails. You may make around 10,000 rupees per month through this. You are paid anywhere between 20 paise to 200 rupees for reading one email. For this, you need to log in to your account every day and read emails in the inbox. If you get one of your friends to open his account here, you are paid up to 100 rupees for the same.

Become a Consultant

You may earn money by sharing your knowledge with people. You don't have to be a great scholar for this, but you certainly need to be knowing more than the person you are trying to counsel.

Earn through Social Media

If you have some negative thinking with regard to making money on social media, you may be entirely wrong, as there are many people today who have a huge number of followers on social media and they charge fees up to 20,000 rupees for publishing a single post. Many a time, they charge even more than that, and the most important point here is that this earning comes from the followers on social media. That is, the more the number of their followers, the more would be the earning through social media Apps.

Online Games

This is the age of computers. Today, innumerable people across the world are making millions through Online games. There were computer games earlier also, but you were not able to earn money out of the same. Times have changed now. It's easy to earn now just by playing games. An Online game is thus a very good medium. The number of Online game players is growing very fast. You also may take advantage of this opportunity and make money while having fun.

It's not that easy to become a 'super player' in computer games; this requires a lot of practice and sharp brain. The way to make money through Online games is—to keep playing and keep winning. Today, there are thousands of Online games where you can earn money. Some of such games are EasyGames, GameDuell, Skillz, Rummy, and Multiplayer Card Games.

'Rummy' is also one of those games where you may make money. You receive a good bonus in the same and you are paid money separately as well. New offers in the same keep coming every day.

Another Online game is Multiplayer Card Games. You may earn money here also. You may download this from Google on your phone or computer. Multiplayer Card Games is a great means of making money and is also full of fun.

Similarly, there are plenty of other Online games that offer you the opportunity to earn money. You have to play these games very diligently. If you play the games very diligently and with full application of mind, you are sure to make money. You should first understand the game thoroughly, check related offers, play trials, and then after you have a clear understanding of the game, make money with ease. Keep playing and keep earning. As you keep getting a better understanding of the game, your income would keep increasing. Online games, while being entertaining, are also good income opportunities. They sharpen your mind, improve your concentration and enhance your capacity to face challenges.

❑